AF407453

Li'l Eddie Moves to the Farm

Mary Griffith Chalupsky

Published and Copyright 2022 by Corridor Publishing

marygriffithchalupskybooks.bigcartel.com

mary.chalupsky@yahoo.com

Special discounts are available on quantity purchases by corporations, schools, libraries, charities and others. For information on special discounts email the author at

mary.chalupsky@yahoo.com

Illustrator Mohsen Abdelhafiz

LI'L EDDIE
MOVES TO THE FARM

Author: Mary Griffith Chalupsky

Illustrator: Mohsen Abdelhafiz

Dedication

To Edward 'Eddie' Chalupsky, one of six of my best friends in the whole, wide world. With an apology to the children who read it, 'Eddie,' like Li'l Eddie in this book, was quite a little terror. He was the youngest child and he gave me more grey hairs than I cared for, but, he grew up to be a good man.

So this book is dedicated to 'Eddie' as a child, who constantly was a challenge every day of his 'little' boy life.

Love, Mom

Li'l Eddie could hear his Mama and Daddy talking about moving to the farm.They were talking about big trucks, movers,and Grandma and Grandpa who would be left behind until their little house in the meadow was painted.

Li'l Eddie started screaming! "I don't wanna move! I like it here! I like my bedroom, my toys, my bed, my yard! I don't wanna move! I don't wanna move! Please, I don't wanna go!" he yelled as he lay on the floor kicking and screaming as loud as he could.

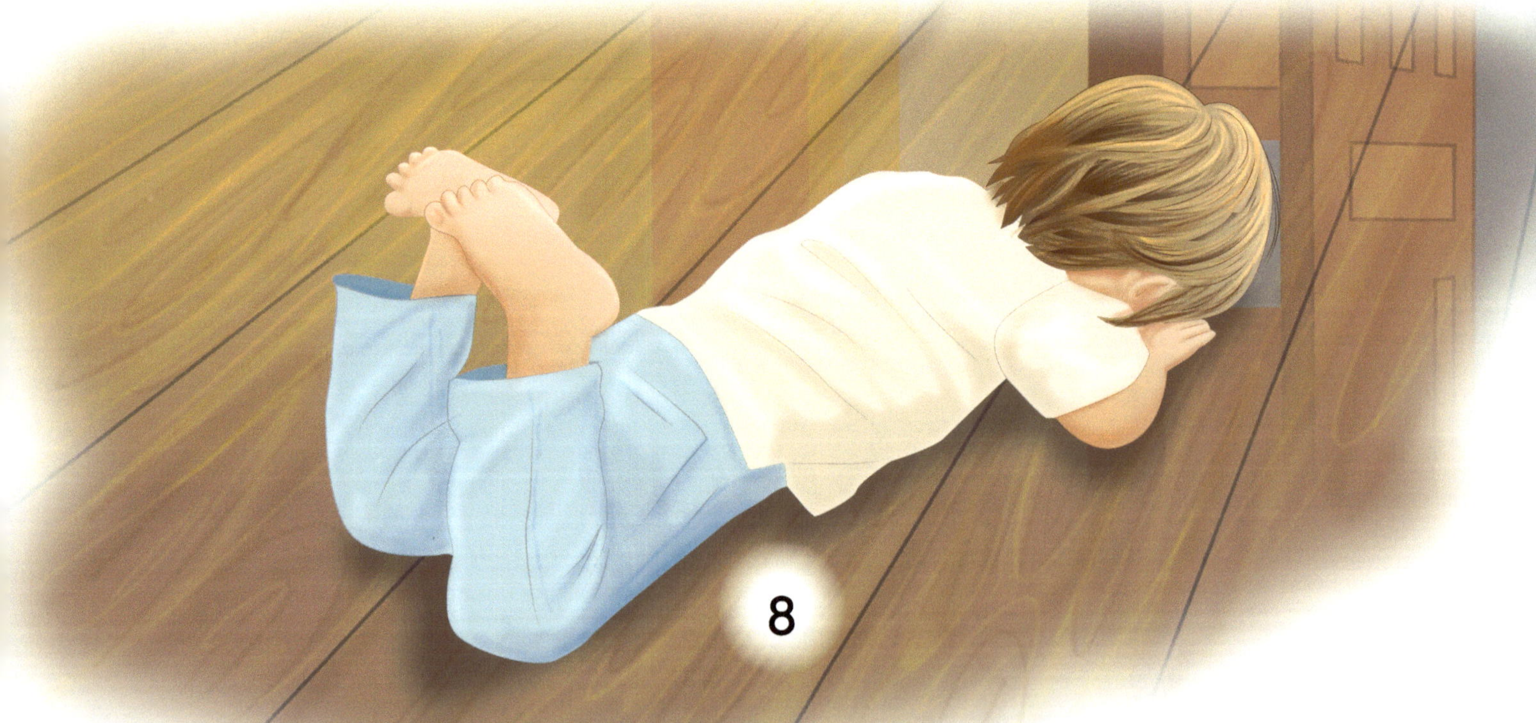

Willy, his little black dog, looked at him and hid
under the bed. Willy didn't know what to think.

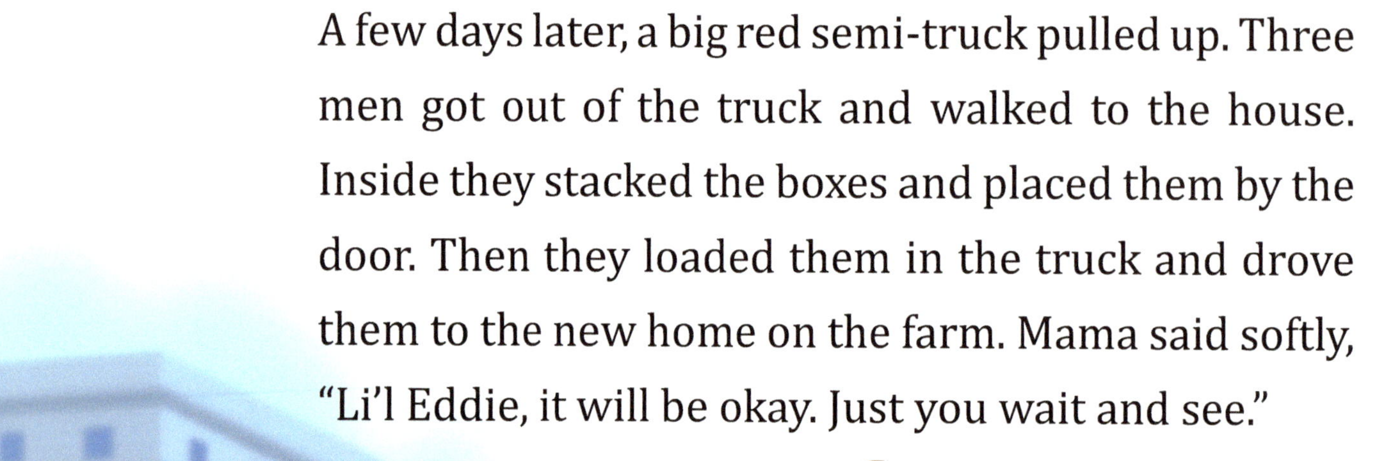

A few days later, a big red semi-truck pulled up. Three men got out of the truck and walked to the house. Inside they stacked the boxes and placed them by the door. Then they loaded them in the truck and drove them to the new home on the farm. Mama said softly, "Li'l Eddie, it will be okay. Just you wait and see."

After the men unloaded the boxes,
they drove away.

Li'l Eddie wiped his tears on his shirt sleeve and looked around.
He could see many things; a big barn, shed, chicken coop, a big
tractor and a pond. Li'l Eddie ran to the big barn and opened
the door. Inside were goats, four horses, and two cows.

They were making funny noises. Some of the goats were big and some were little. Some had big horns and some had little horns. Some had beards and some had spots.

Li'l Eddie played with the goats for a while, then he left the barn and ran to the chicken house. He could see chickens walking around the chicken yard. They were scratching in the dirt. Some were eating grain.

Others were drinking from chicken waterers. There were many kinds of chickens; red ones, black ones, white ones, spotted ones, and some with fluffy feathers on the top of their heads and their feet.

Li'l Eddie loved them all.
He played with them for a long time. Then he decided to check the tractor by the shed.

He climbed up on the tractor seat and stretched his legs to see if he could touch the gas pedal.

16

He couldn't, so he sat on the seat and pretended he was driving by turning the steering wheel back and forth. *Pft…Pft…* voom… he blew with his lips, trying to sound like a motor running. *Pft…Pft…Pft…*voom… Li'l Eddie was having a great time.

In the city, he didn't have a tractor. He didn't have a barn with goats, cows and horses, and he didn't have a chicken coop with chickens. He didn't have a pond with fish jumping all over, a nice place to sit where he could catch fish for dinner, or a pond he could swim in the summer time.

Li'l Eddie hopped down off the tractor and ran to the pond. He could see ducks and geese swimming, and once in a while, a fish would leap in the air.

He decided to take off his shoes and go wading. It was a nice, warm day and what could it hurt? He started walking in the sand around the pond.
Soon his toes were squishing with mud.
It was slippery, so after a few steps, his feet slipped

out from under him and he fell. The water completely covered him. Willy was barking, and Li'l Eddie was yelling for his Daddy.

22

Daddy heard the commotion. He jumped in the pond and pulled him out. It was an exciting moment, even though it was scary.

Daddy said,"Li'l Eddie, how many times must I tell you not to go near the pond unless someone is with you? It isn't safe and you could drown. There is a lot to see on the farm, so please stay away from the pond until you are with an adult. Even then, I want to know where you are. It is so easy to slip beneath the water where no one can see you. Please promise me that you will listen to me about the pond."

"Okay Dad, I promise," replied Li'l Eddie as he ran off to see what else he could find to do.

Li'l Eddie looked around and he could see vast corn fields and nothing more in the distance. He breathed deeply as he muttered beneath his breath.

"There are no neighbors. I have no friends here. Just the pigs, chickens, goats, horses and cows. What on earth am I to do? I'll never get through a day without playing with my friends."

25

He hung his head and continued to walk around in circles thinking. Mama yelled! "Li'l Eddie, time for dinner! Come wash your hands!"

Li'l Eddie shuffled into the bathroom, washed his hands and headed for the kitchen.

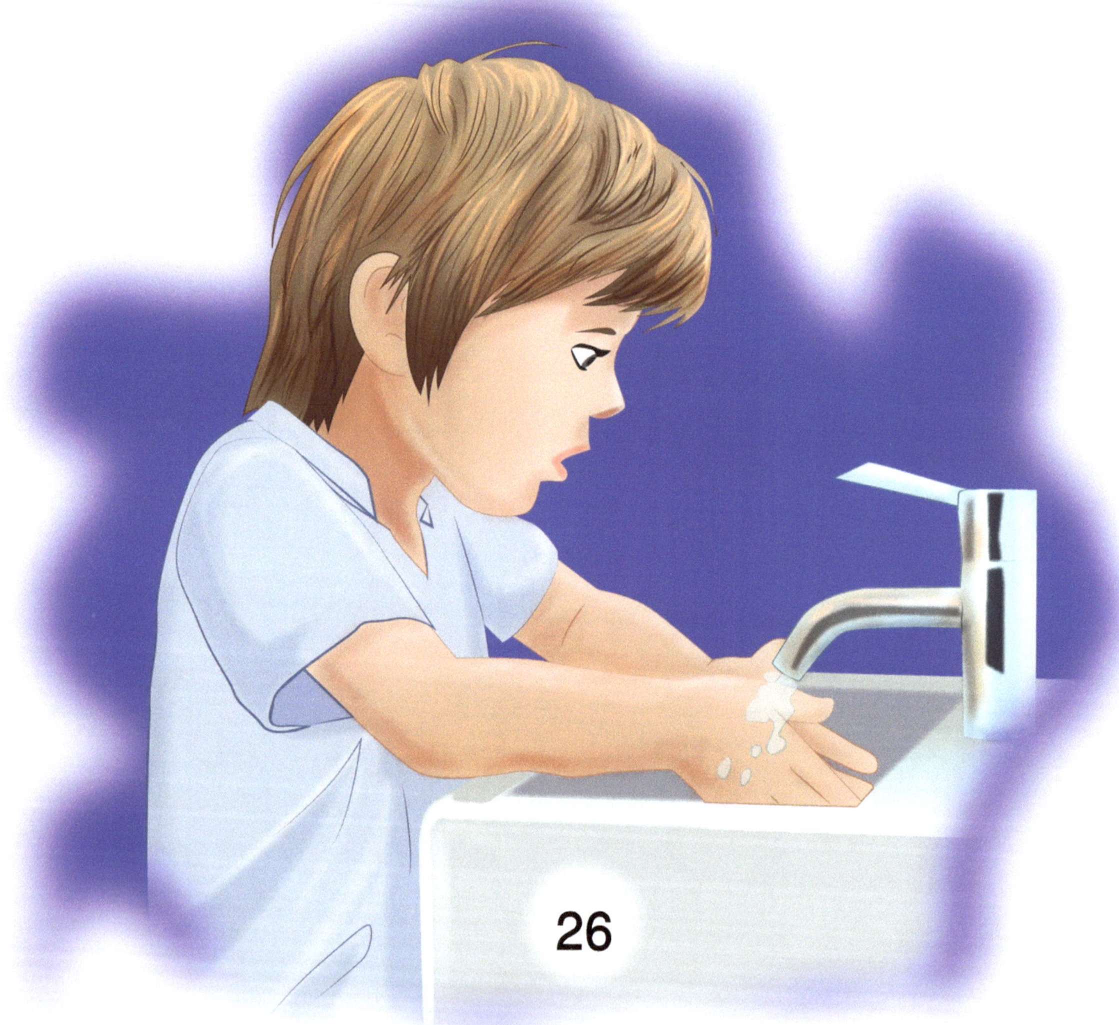

26

Bowing their heads, Daddy said the blessing and they all ate quietly. Many questions were forming in Li'l Eddie's mind, but they were jumbled as much as his meat and mashed potatoes in his mouth. He ate quickly because he wanted to see the animals one more time before he went to bed.

He already knew he had many more friends than he ever had before. He would have friends at school and friends at home. He was so happy he smiled from ear to ear.

He hurried outside to say goodnight to the goats, cows, chickens, horses, pigs, and to the fish in the pond.

Then he went inside, brushed his teeth, and he and Willy went to bed. Closing his eyes, he could still see all of his farm friends, the animals, waiting for him at the gate. He had many friends after all. It will be so much fun living on the farm.

Li'l Eddie smiled as he fell sound asleep knowing tomorrow would be a wonderful day.

Coloring Page

Coloring Page

BIOGRAPHY
Mary Griffith Chalupsky

Mary Griffith Chalupsky grew up in a little town in southern Illinois. She and her husband raised six children on a farm in central Iowa.

She won several awards during her lifetime through the World Poetry Association beginning in 1987 when she won the Golden Poet Award, the Silver Poet Award followed in 1990, and the Editor choice Award in 2005, 2006, and 2007.

Mary was a volunteer in her church, school and community for most of her life. She worked in the medical profession and owned and operated her own business, Medical Claims Billing. She is a member of the DAR and the Mayflower Society.

Presently she lives in Cedar Rapids, Iowa with her little dog Buttons, and she loves sitting on her back porch, working in her flower gardens and having coffee with her friends.

Mohsen Abdel Hafeez Abdel Aal
Biography

Mohsen Abdel Hafeez Abdel Aal, an Egyptian journalist and artist is interested in writing and illustrating children's books. He is the author of more than 1000 books published in Egypt, the UAE, Saudi Arabia, Morocco, The United States and The United Kingdom, in Arabic and English languages. He is interested in communicating between different cultures, respect for humanity and love for the diverse animals with which we share the same environment.

This is the 5th book he has illustrated for author Mary Griffith Chalupsky.

Books By
Mary Griffith Chalupsky

JOGGER'S ADVENTURES

How Jogger Got His Name

Jogger Goes to School

Jogger Learns to Fish

Jogger Goes to the Circus

Christmas With Jogger

Jogger's Valentines

Jogger Drives Big Red

Jogger Goes to the Prom

Jogger Saves the Day

Jogger's New Friends

Jogger Goes to a Car Show

Jogger Goes to a Rodeo

Jogger's Birthday

A Bicycle for Jogger

Fun at the Amusement Park

The Littlest Puppy

Jimmy's Adventures

The Big, Bad, Sad, Mad Meany

Wings, Fins, a Bully and Friends, Book 1, 2

Puppy Pirates

Finding Christmas Spirit

Mary's Garden (a book of original poetry)

Tales from the Enchanted Forest, book 1, 2,3

Beyond the Rainbow Bridge

Mali, the Therapy Dog

The Naughty Rotties